Children's Illustrators

Chris Van Allsburg

Jill C. Wheeler
ABDO Publishing Company

visit us at
www.abdopub.com

Published by ABDO Publishing Company, 4940 Viking Drive, Edina, Minnesota 55435.
Copyright © 2005 by Abdo Consulting Group, Inc. International copyrights reserved in all
countries. No part of this book may be reproduced in any form without written permission from
the publisher. The Checkerboard Library™ is a trademark and logo of ABDO Publishing
Company.

Printed in the United States.

Cover Photo: AP/Wide World
Interior Photos: AP/Wide World p. 6; Getty Images pp. 5, 10, 12, 19, 21, 23; Houghton Mifflin
    pp. 7, 17; Kerlan Collection, University of Minnesota Libraries pp. 9, 15

Series Coordinator: Jennifer R. Krueger
Editors: Heidi M. Dahmes, Jennifer R. Krueger
Art Direction: Neil Klinepier

Library of Congress Cataloging-in-Publication Data

Wheeler, Jill C., 1964-
    Chris Van Allsburg / Jill C. Wheeler.
       p. cm. -- (Children's illustrators)
    Includes bibliographical references and index.
    ISBN 1-59197-721-5
       1. Van Allsburg, Chris--Juvenile literature. 2. Illustrators--United States--Biography--
Juvenile literature. I. Title.

NC975.5.V36W57 2004
741.6'42'092--dc22

                                                                      2004046294

38888000052740

Contents

Nothing Quite Like It

Take an ordinary object. Put it in an unexpected place, and add a touch of mystery. Such is the world of author and illustrator Chris Van Allsburg. Van Allsburg is the creator of such popular books as *Jumanji* and *The Polar Express*. Van Allsburg's artwork can look very realistic. It can also hold an element of wonder.

Van Allsburg's award-winning work has been featured in galleries and movies, as well as books. His dreamlike artwork creates an amazing world where ordinary objects become mysterious. His illustrations create a place where most anything can happen and often does.

Van Allsburg began his art career in sculpture. His sculpting background can be seen in the style of his drawings. Readers cannot help but stop and gaze at the illustrations to take in the full effect. No matter what the medium, his art weaves a rich and sometimes haunting story.

Van Allsburg illustrates mostly his own books. But,
he has also provided illustrations for the projects of
other authors, such as Mark Helprin's Swan Lake.
As in his other books, Van Allsburg's art for Swan
Lake is enjoyed by adults and children alike.

Growing Up in Michigan

    Chris Van Allsburg was born on June 18, 1949, in Grand Rapids, Michigan, to Richard and Chris Van Allsburg. Richard owned a dairy. Later, he opened an ice cream parlor that Chris's mother ran. Chris also had an older sister named Karen.

    The area around Grand Rapids was changing from rural to **suburban** when Chris lived there as a child. More and more houses were built where there used to be fields. Chris and his friends enjoyed exploring the houses under construction. They also liked sledding and riding their bicycles.

Dagwood Bumstead is part of the Blondie comic strip.

THE POLAR EXPRESS

As a child, Van Allsburg especially enjoyed building model trains. A ride on a steam train is the focal point of one of his most popular books.

At home, Chris liked to build models. He built model cars, trucks, and planes. He painted them very carefully. He could easily draw popular cartoon characters such as Mickey Mouse, Pluto, Dagwood Bumstead, and Pogo. Those drawings often delighted his fellow students.

By fifth grade, Chris recalls, some students considered artistic talent to be kind of nerdy. He spent less time drawing and more time pursuing other activities. Chris remembers playing baseball, reading *Mad* magazine, and playing board games such as Clue and Life.

Chris was not sure what to do after graduating from East Grand Rapids High School. He briefly considered becoming a lawyer. But at the University of Michigan in Ann Arbor, he decided to take some art classes.

Most of the other art students had already spent years studying art, especially drawing. They also had many samples of their work. School officials did not seem to care that Chris had not taken many art classes in high school. Neither did they care that he had no **portfolio** of work.

Chris began at the university in 1967. He found himself enjoying art, as he had as a child. He did some drawing, but he especially enjoyed sculpting. He learned he had a natural talent for making sculptures. Many of his sculptures seemed to have a story behind them.

Opposite Page: *Van Allsburg thought earning an art degree would be a fun way to spend the next four years.*

Chris learned how to work with bronze, wood, and **ceramics**. He found that art school was actually a lot of work. Some studio classes lasted an entire day. His four years stretched into five.

Mastering Sculpture

At the university, Van Allsburg began dating a student named Lisa Morrison. After graduation, the couple moved to Providence, Rhode Island. Van Allsburg spent two years at the Rhode Island School of Design (RISD). He earned his master's degree in art in 1975. He then began teaching at RISD.

Lisa was by now his wife and his **representative**. She helped arrange for him to exhibit his work at a New York City gallery. Other gallery connections later helped Van Allsburg place several drawings at the Whitney Museum of American Art.

Van Allsburg still loved sculpting. Yet, sculpting required a special place to work. Van Allsburg's studio was in an old brick building that was usually cold. He decided to do more work that did not require a studio. He began to draw in the evenings.

One day Lisa was looking through his drawings. She thought children would enjoy them. Lisa had met an artist who wrote and illustrated children's books. His name was David Macaulay.

Macaulay arranged for Lisa to show his editor examples of Van Allsburg's work. The editor proposed that Van Allsburg illustrate books written by other people. After he met Van Allsburg, the editor encouraged him to write his own stories.

Opposite Page: *Van Allsburg (right) visits a RISD class. He was not sculpting as much because of the time he spent at RISD. However, he was still drawing at home in the evening.*

Books as Art

It did not take long for Van Allsburg to realize that he preferred writing his own stories. He created a story about a boy who follows a lost dog into the garden of a retired magician. The magician's lavish home and garden come to life in incredibly detailed, black-and-white drawings.

The Garden of Abdul Gasazi was published by Houghton Mifflin in 1979. Van Allsburg thought his book might sell just a

few copies. However, it went on to sell many. Critics took note of the high standard of the artwork. The book was even named a **Caldecott Honor Book**.

Although his first three books were in black and white, Van Allsburg would later have success illustrating in color.

Van Allsburg was pleased with how well the book did. However, he had no plans to continue creating children's books. He went back to sculpting. But, writing the book had changed the way he thought about his sculpting projects. He began to see stories behind all of his artwork.

Elements of Art

Composition

Composition is one of the basic parts of art. It is the arrangement of forms, lines, and colors within the frame of the picture. Composition plays a big role in how a finished picture looks and feels.

For Van Allsburg, composition is the most enjoyable part of illustrating. He likes to move objects around and decide what size they should be. Van Allsburg spent a long time determining the composition of his *Jumanji* illustrations. In the end, many of the compositions create an unsettling and mysterious image.

Jumanji

It was not long before Van Allsburg was imagining another story. This was the story of two bored kids who decide to play a board game. It is a jungle game where the events actually happen in real life! The children end up with a house full of wild animals.

Van Allsburg had seen jungle animals before in the zoo. However, he had not seen them inside a house. He used plastic or clay figures to help him draw. He also hung photos of animals a long way from where he was working. That made the pictures a little fuzzy, so it was easier to imagine the scenes.

Jumanji was published in 1981. Like his first book, it featured elegant black-and-white illustrations with an amazing level of detail. Also like his first book, *Jumanji* captured the attention of the **Caldecott Medal** judges. Only this time, it won the medal.

Opposite Page: *Van Allsburg's sketches for* Jumanji.
*Much of the time that Van Allsburg spends on a book
is for the many rounds of drawing required.*

Jumanji became a feature film starring Robin Williams in 1995. Van Allsburg was a little disappointed with the movie at first. He had hoped his story would become something odd and mysterious. Instead, it turned out to be an action-adventure tale. But, he still thinks the movie held on to his original ideas.

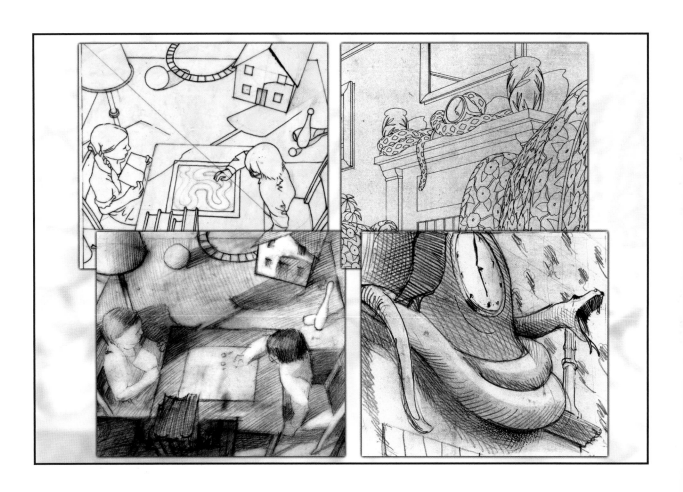

A Second Caldecott

Van Allsburg did a third book in black and white called *Ben's Dream*. His next book, *The Wreck of the Zephyr,* was his first in full color. Van Allsburg returned to black-and-white illustrations with *The Mysteries of Harris Burdick*.

Van Allsburg's next project was *The Polar Express*. This is the story of a boy's special Christmas memory. *The Polar Express* captured a **Caldecott Medal** in 1986.

Van Allsburg published *The Stranger* that same year and *The Z Was Zapped* in 1987. He then wrote and illustrated *Two Bad Ants*. Van Allsburg's next project was a **collaboration** with writer Mark Helprin. Van Allsburg did the illustrations for Helprin's retelling of *Swan Lake*.

Van Allsburg stayed busy in the following years. He and his wife had two daughters. And, he continued writing and illustrating. He completed five books within six years. He

Opposite Page: *When* **The Polar Express** *won the Caldecott Medal in 1986, Van Allsburg became one of only a handful of illustrators to earn two Caldecott Medals.*

followed those with two more projects with Helprin titled *A City in Winter* and *The Veil of Snows*.

His fans had to wait five years for his next project. Yet, the space adventure *Zathura* proved to be worth the wait. It was a **sequel** to *Jumanji* published 20 years later. *Zathura* landed on the bestseller list even before its official release.

A Lonely Job

Van Allsburg says being an artist can be a lonely job. He often works eight to nine hours a day at his **antique drafting** table. The table sits in his studio in Providence. Most of the time he works alone. He does take some time away from work to read, take walks, or play tennis.

It takes Van Allsburg about four to seven months to create a new book. A typical picture book contains 14 to 15 drawings. Van Allsburg says he begins to get tired by about the tenth illustration. By that time, he is excited to start a different project. Readers are always interested, however.

Part of the appeal of Van Allsburg's art comes from its mysterious quality. He uses **perspective**, light, and **point of view** to add a touch of mystery. He also works in a variety of mediums including pencil, **charcoal**, pen and ink, pastels, and watercolor.

Van Allsburg works alone in his home studio.

Even everyday objects can be a source of wonder for Van Allsburg. As a child, he loved to build models. He still uses models sometimes to help with his illustrations. A model gives him a **three-dimensional** view of an object. It helps him see where shadows would fall.

On the Big Screen Again

Van Allsburg continues to work to bring his illustrations to life. He has worked with actor Tom Hanks and director Robert Zemeckis to bring *The Polar Express* to the big screen.

The movie is the first feature film to use the new motion-capture process for every character. This process uses special machines to capture live actors' movements and the emotions they convey. Those movements are then put into a computer and mixed with computer-generated environments.

The Polar Express will come to theaters in 2004. As for what lies beyond, Van Allsburg does not yet know. He has ideas for more books and has been approached about making movies from several of his other books. Whatever his next project, Van Allsburg can be sure his fans are waiting.

Opposite Page: *Van Allsburg and his daughter, Sophia. He says his daughters are proud of his work. However, he adds, they do not seem too excited about the fact that their father is a famous artist.*

Glossary

antique - an old item that has collectible value.

Caldecott Medal - an award the American Library Association gives to the artist who illustrated the year's best picture book. Runners-up are called Caldecott Honor Books.

ceramic - baked clay.

charcoal - a soft, black material used in pencils.

collaborate - to work together.

draft - a sketch or design. Drafting tables are used by artists as a surface on which to draw.

perspective - the art of giving objects drawn on a flat surface the illusion of being three-dimensional.

point of view - the position from which something is seen, such as from above or below.

portfolio - a portable case holding a collection of an artist's work for display.

representative - a person who shows the work of artists or writers to possible customers and publishers.

sequel - a book or movie continuing a story that began previously.

suburb - the towns or villages just outside a city.

three-dimensional - related to having three dimensions or to having the illusion of depth.

Web Sites

To learn more about Chris Van Allsburg, visit ABDO Publishing Company on the World Wide Web at **www.abdopub.com**. Web sites about Chris Van Allsburg are featured on our Book Links page. These links are routinely monitored and updated to provide the most current information available.

Index